ROYAL COURT

Royal Court Theatre presents

CREDIBLE WITNESS

by **Timberlake Wertenbaker**

First performance at the Royal Court Jerwood Theatre Upstairs,
Sloane Square, London on 8 February 2001.

CREDIBLE WITNESS

by **Timberlake Wertenbaker**

Cast in order of appearance
Alexander Karagy **Adam Kotz**
Petra Karagy **Olympia Dukakis**
Paul **Paul Bhattacharjee**
Anna **Tea Agbaba**
Ali **Yusuf Altin**
Henry **Benjamin Boateng**
Aziz **Anthony Barclay**
Ameena **Leona Ekembe**
Shivan **Vincent Ebrahim**
Leon **Roland John-Leopoldie**
Simon **Clive Merrison**

Director **Sacha Wares**
Designer **Es Devlin**
Lighting Designer **Paule Constable**
Sound Designer **Fergus O'Hare for Aura**
Composer **Adrian Lee**
Assistant Director **Simon Green**
Assistant Designer **Lisa Lillywhite**
Casting Director **Lisa Makin**
Production Manager **Sue Bird**
Company Stage Manager **Cath Binks**
Stage Management **Sharon Cooper, Leila Jones**
Stage Management Work Placement **Emma Goodway**
Costume Supervisor **Fizz Jones**
Dialect Coaching **Jeannette Nelson & Tim Charrington**
Company Voice Work **Patsy Rodenburg**
Set Construction **www.andybeauchamp.co.uk**

Royal Court Theatre would like to thank the many people who helped with this production including:
Catherine Bailey, Helen Bamber at Medical Foundation for Victims of Torture, Boris Boskovic, Ruth Davey
at Refugee Council, Elyse Dodgson, Rebecca Gatward, Tesfay Gebremichael, Dr Basil C Gounaris,
Pippa Harrison at Spotlight, Hilary Hazzard, Demetra Hersey, Glynis Jones, Penelope Kombothekra at the
British Council in Athens, Professor Vassilis Kontis, Emily Man, Slavko Mangovski, Bill McAlister, Sue Mayo,
Madlena Nedeva, Chrysoula Nelidou at the British Council in Thessaloniki, Rosamond Perrott, Isabelle
at London Detainee Support Group, Kumar at Tamil Information Centre, Indhu Rubasingham, Sadia,
Dr Sekhou at Algerian Refugee Council, Bosnian Institute, Eleni Valtadorou, Sladjana Vujovic, Lewis Wolpert.
Special thanks to Lindsay Posner, Rufus Norris, Brana Bajic, Danny Cerqueira, Kathryn Hunter, Lennie James
and Joy Richardson for their participation in the 1997 Refugee Research Project.
Wardrobe care by Persil and Comfort courtesy of Lever Brothers Ltd.

THE COMPANY

Timberlake Wertenbaker (writer)
For the Royal Court: Abel's Sister, The Grace of
Mary Traverse, Our Country's Good, Three Birds
Alighting on a Field, The Break of Day (with Out of
Joint).
Other theatre includes: Case to Answer (Soho
Poly); New Anatomies (ICA); The Love of the
Nightingale (RSC); After Darwin (Hampstead); The
Ash Girl (Birmingham Rep).
Translations include: False Admissions, Successful
Strategies (Shared Experience); Mephisto, The
Thebans (RSC); Hecuba (ACT); Filumena (West
End).
Screenplays include: The Children, Do Not
Disturb.
Radio includes: La Dispute (translation); Leocadia
(translation); Pelleas and Melisande (translation);
Madame Paradis, Dianeira.

Tea Agbaba
Credible Witness is Tea's first professional
production.

Yusuf Altin
Television includes: Alistair McGowan, Privates, Red
Alert – National Lottery, Real Women, Spaced,
Psychos, Stuart.
Film includes: My Other Wheelchair is a Porsche,
Esther Khan, Magic Seed, BT Talk Walk.

Anthony Barclay
Theatre includes: Ticket to Write (West Yorkshire
Playhouse / Paines Plough); Vurt (Contact); Taming
of the Shrew (English Touring Theatre); Line (King's
Head); Assassins (Donmar Warehouse); The Iron
Man, In the Midnight Hour (Young Vic); Children of
Eden (Prince Edward); Julius Caesar, The
Fantasticks (Open Air, Regents Park); Just So
(Watermill); Follies (Shaftesbury); Pacific Overtures,
Blood Brothers, Trumpets and Raspberries (Library,
Manchester).
Television includes: Lock, Stock, Smack the Pony,
Dream Team, Birds of a Feather, Casualty, The Bill,
Common as Muck, Sorry About Last Night,
Screaming, Love Hurts, Bob and Margaret,
Watership Down.
Film includes: Prix de Rome.
Radio includes: Sorry About Last Night.

Paul Bhattacharjee
For the Royal Court: Iranian Nights, Lalita's
Way, Mohair, The Burrow (Young
Writers' Festival), Blood.
Other theatre includes: Arabian Nights (world
tour for Young Vic); Twelfth Night (US tour);
Seagull, Present Laughter, The Tempest, A
Perfect Ganesh (West Yorkshire Playhouse);
Aureng-Zebe (RNT Studio); Indian Ink
(Aldwych); Fashion (Tricycle); Murmuring
Judges (RNT); Yes, Memsahib, Inkalaab 1919,
Sacrifice, The Lion's Raj, Ancestral Voices,
Meet Me, Chilli in Your Eyes, Bicharo
(National tour); Your England (Riverside
Studios); The Little Clay Cart (Tara Arts); The
Broken Thigh (Drill Hall); Exile in the Forest
(The Place); Sweet Dreams (Urban Turbans).
Television includes: Hawk, Navy in Action,
Thieftakers, Wing and a Prayer, Turning
World, Two Oranges and a Mango, The Bill,
Inkallaab, Ancestral Voices, Chilli in Your Eyes,
Johnny Jarvis, Pravina's Wedding, Maigret,
Albion Market, Lovebirds, Shalom Salaam,
Bergerac, Here is the News, Saracen,
Northern Crescent, Black and Blue, Clubland,
Sister Wife, A Summer Day's Dream.
Film includes: Jinnah, Wild West.

Benjamin Boateng
Theatre includes: Whistle Down the Wind
(Aldwych).
Television includes: Grange Hill, Toonatics,
Crime Watch.
Recording includes: The original cast
recording of Whistle Down the Wind.

Paule Constable (lighting designer)
For the Royal Court: The Country, Dublin
Carol, The Weir, The Glory of Living.
Other theatre includes: The Seagull, Tales
from Ovid, The Dispute, Uncle Vanya,
Beckett Shorts, The Mysteries (RSC); The
Villains' Opera, Darker Face of the Earth,
Haroun and the Sea of Stories, Caucasian
Chalk Circle (RNT); Amadeus (West End,
Broadway, Olivier nomination); Les Miserables
(Tel Aviv); Playhouse Creatures (Old Vic);
More Grimms' Tales (Young Vic and New
York); four productions for Theatre de
Complicite including the Olivier nominated
Street of Crocodiles.
Opera includes: productions for the English
National Opera, Welsh National Opera,
Scottish Opera, Opera North, Glyndebourne,
La Monnaie.

Es Devlin (designer)

For the Royal Court: Yard Gal (with Clean Break).

Theatre includes: Yard Gal (MCC Theatre, New York); Meat (Theatre Royal, Plymouth); Rita, Sue and Bob Too, A State Affair (Out of Joint, Soho, Liverpool Everyman and tour); Henry IV parts I &II (RSC); Pera Palas (RNT Studio / Gate); One Life and Counting, Drink, Dance, Laugh and Lie, Love You Too, Love and Understanding (Bush/ Long Wharf Theatre, USA); Hamlet (Young Vic, Theatre Royal Plymouth and Tokyo Globe); Howie the Rookie (Bush); Betrayal (RNT); Snake in the Grass (Peter Hall Co at the Old Vic); Piano (Theatre Project, Tokyo); Edward II (Octagon, Bolton); Wizard of Oz (National Youth Music Theatre).

Opera includes: National Opera Studio 1999 Showcase (Queen Elizabeth Hall); Powder Her Face (Ystad Festival, Sweden); Fidelio (English Touring Opera); Don Giovanni (British Youth Opera), Live Culture (ENO Works).

Film includes: Brilliant, Snow on Saturday, Beggars Belief, A Tale of Two Heads.

Dance includes: God's Plenty, Four Scenes (Rambert).

Awards include: Barclays TMA Best Designer 1999 for Howie the Rookie, Linbury prize for Stage Design 1995/6.

Olympia Dukakis

Theatre includes: Rose (RNT, Broadway); Hecuba, The Singer's Boy (American Conservatory Theater); Lear and Her Daughters (Orpheum Theatre); The Hope Zone (Circle Repertory Theatre); The Marriage of Bette and Boo, Curse Of the Starving Class (Public Theater); Baby Goya (American Place Theatre); Peer Gynt, Titus Andronicus, Electra (New York Shakespeare Festival); Social Security, A View From the Bridge, Night of the Iguana, The Aspern Papers, Who's Who in Hell (Broadway) Agamemnon, A Man's a Man, The New Tenant, Crimes and Crimes (Off Broadway).

Television includes: A Life for a Life, Joan of Arc, More Tales of the City, Scattering Dad, The Pentagon Wars, A Match Made in Heaven, Hoboken, A Century of Women, Tales of the City, Sinatra, A Fire in the Dark, The Last Act is Solo, Lucky Day.

Film includes: Moonstruck, Steel Magnolias, Look Who's Talking I, II, & III, Dad, Mr. Holland's Opus, Jerusalem, Picture Perfect, Mighty Aphrodite, Better Living, Mafia!, Jeffrey, I Love Trouble, In The Spirit, Working Girl.

Awards include: Academy Award Best Supporting Actress, Golden Globe Award, National Board of Review, LA Film Critics, Comedy Award for Moonstruck, Outer Circle Critics award for Rose, OBIE award for The Marriage of Bette and Boo, OBIE award for Man's a Man, Theatre World Award for A View From the Bridge, Cable ACE Award, Best Actress for The Last Act is Solo.

Vincent Ebrahim

For the Royal Court: Minor Complications, Borderline (with Joint Stock).

Other theatre includes: The Ramayana (Birmingham Rep); Aureng-Zebe (RNT Studio); Across the Black Waters (Man Mela); Orpheus (ATC); Little Clay Cart, Fanshen (RNT); Oh Sweet Sita, A Midsummer Night's Dream, The Bourgeios Gentilhomme, Oedipus the King, Troilus and Cressida, Antigone and the Government Inspector (Tara Arts); Tartuffe, Cyrano (Tara Arts and RNT); Promised Land (Joint Stock); Real Dreams, The Danton Affair (RSC); Julius Caesar (Young Vic); Woyzeck, Medea, George Dandin (Leicester Haymarket Studio); Turning Over (West Yorkshire Playhouse); The Guest Room (Old Red Lion).

Radio includes: The Truck, The Eternal Bubble, What Now, Now that we are Dead?, Harvest, The Cyclist, The Book of Secrets, Vital Signs, Like Another Mahabharata, The Dreams of Tippu Sultan, Scorching Winds, Song of my Father.

Leona Ekembe

Credible Witness is Leona's first professional production.

Simon Green (assistant director)

Theatre as director includes: Don Giovanni (Cambridge Arts Centre); Slag (Finborough). Theatre as assistant director includes: Art (Wyndham's); Saved by Sex (Edinburgh Fringe); Family Viewing, Crimes of the Heart (King's Head).

Roland John-Leopoldie

Theatre includes: Imoinda (Hornimann Museum); Les Gens des Marais (The Swamp Dwellers) (Maison d'Orgement).

Film includes: Tout-contre.

Adam Kotz

For the Royal Court: Royal Borough, Ambulance.

Other theatre includes: War Play Trilogy, Love's Labour's Lost (RSC); True Dare Kiss, Command or Promise, Racing Demon, The Miser, Le Bourgeois Gentilhomme, Trelawny of the Wells, Murmuring Judges, The Prime of Miss Jean Brodie (RNT); Romeo and Juliet, Spring Awakening, Leonce and Lena (Sheffield Crucible); No Pasaran (Young Vic); Hamlet, Gotcha (Dukes, Lancaster); Watching (Bush/Liverpool Playhouse); The Freud Scenario, Dealer's Choice (RNT Studio); A Family Affair, Measure for Measure (Cheek By Jowl); A Midsummer Night's Dream (Manchester Royal Exchange); The Ghost Sonata (The Opera Factory); As You Like It (Old Vic); 1953 (Almeida).

Television includes: Never Never, Anchor Me, Monsignor Renard, All the King's Men, Mr White Goes to Westminster, Touching Evil, Out of the Blue II, Band of Gold, Symmetry, Dangerfield, Casualty, The Bill, Wycliffe, Asylum War, Brookside, Moving Story, Heartbeat, The Mushroom Picker, The Big Battalions, Poirot, East of the Moon, The South Bank Show, Bulman, Miracles Take Longer, Juliet Bravo, The Practice, Driving Ambition, Tuckers Luck, Oi for England.

Forthcoming television includes: The Whistleblower, Perfect.

Film includes: Love Potion No 9, Without a Clue, Max and Helen, Shot Through the Heart, Out of the Blue.

Radio includes regular recordings for BBC and independents.

Adrian Lee (composer)

Theatre includes: Romeo and Juliet, Haroun and the Sea of Stories, A Midsummer Night's Dream, Gilgamesh, The Little Clay Cart (RNT); Macbeth, Tales from Ovid, The Comedy of Errors (RSC); Viel Lärm Um Nichts (Maxim Gorki Theater, Berlin); Grimms' Tales, The Jungle Book, Blood Wedding, More Grimms' Tales, Twelfth Night, As I Lay Dying (Young Vic); A Midsummer Night's Dream(Tara Arts/Lyric, Hammersmith), Pera Pelas (Gate); Dreams of Inanna, Shakti, Itan-Kahani (Pan Projects).

Film includes: Macbeth.

Radio includes: The Little Clay Cart.

CDs include: Grimm Tones for Grimms' Tales, Parallel Life, Music for Comedy of Errors.

Clive Merrison

Theatre includes: The Cocktail Party (Lyceum, Edinburgh); Fair Ladies at a Game of Poem Cards, A Matter of Life and Death (RNT); Reader (Traverse); The Browning Version (Greenwich); The Madness of George III (RNT & US Tour); The Pope and the Witch (Comedy Theatre); Much Ado About Nothing, The Caucasian Chalk Circle, Mephisto, Bastard Angel, Troilus and Cressida, Principia Scriptoriae, Moscow Gold (RSC); Eastwood Ho (Mermaid); Under Milk Wood (Mayfair); The Housekeeper (Queens Theatre); The Possessed (Almeida); Censored Scenes from King Kong, Artaud at Rodez (Open Space); Victoria Wood Revue, The Last Resort, Vampire, Soul of the White Ant (Bush); Macbeth, The Cherry Orchard, Tis Pity She's a Whore, Saturday, Sunday, Monday, The Misanthrope, The Front Page, Richard II (NT at the Old Vic); Luther, Candida (Lyric Belfast); Pygmalion (Birmingham); Travesties (Coventry); Billy Liar (Welsh NT); The Good Woman of Schetzuan, The Madwoman of Chaillot, The Wild Duck, Little Malcolm (Oxford Playhouse).

Television includes: Care, Pie in the Sky, Rebecca's Daughters, Bergerac, Dr Who, Yes Prime Minister, The Round Tower, Tomorrow People, The Bill, McLibel, How Do You Want Me, The Glittering Prizes.

Film includes: The Discovery of Heaven, Pandaemonium, Saving Grace, Janice Beard 45WPM, Up at the Villa, Photographing Fairies, The English Patient, True Blue, An Awfully Big Adventure, Heavenly Creatures, The Sign of Four, Coming Out of the Ice, Firefox, Escape to Victory.

Awards include: Sony Radio Actor of the Year (1984) for Luther.

Fergus O'Hare (sound designer)

For the Royal Court: Backpay, One More Wasted Year, Bazaar, Stranger's House.

Theatre includes: Conversations After a Burial, Cressida, Bash, Our Father, The Jew of Malta (Almeida); Volpone (RSC); Noises Off, The Merchant of Venice, Money, An Enemy of the People, Guiding Star (RNT); Pera Palas, The Odyssey (Gate); John Diamond, A Lump in the Throat (Grace); Merrily We Roll Along, Passion Play (also West End), Juno and the Paycock, The Life of Stuff, Playland, Glengarry Glen Ross, True West, Endgame, Habeas Corpus, The Bullet, How I Learned to Drive, Electra (also Broadway) (Donmar Warehouse); Macbeth (Queen's); Arabian Nights (Young Vic); The Snowman (The Peacock); Starstruck (Tricycle); Yard, Breaking In (Bush); The Death of Cool, By Many Wounds (Hampstead); Dancing at Lughnasa (National Youth Theatre); Pippin, The Golem (Bridewell); Edna-The Spectacle (Haymarket); Orpheus Descending (Donmar Warehouse).

Sacha Wares (director)

Theatre includes: One Life and Counting (Bush); Pera Palas (RNT Studio/Gate); Six Degrees of Separation (Crucible, Sheffield).

Radio includes: Der Kuhhandel.

THE ENGLISH STAGE COMPANY AT THE ROYAL COURT

The English Stage Company at the Royal Court opened in 1956 as a subsidised theatre producing new British plays, international plays and some classical revivals.

The first artistic director George Devine aimed to create a writers' theatre, 'a place where the dramatist is acknowledged as the fundamental creative force in the theatre and where the play is more important than the actors, the director, the designer'. The urgent need was to find a contemporary style in which the play, the acting, direction and design are all combined. He believed that 'the battle will be a long one to continue to create the right conditions for writers to work in'.

Devine aimed to discover 'hard-hitting, uncompromising writers whose plays are stimulating, provocative and exciting'. The Royal Court production of John Osborne's Look Back in Anger in May 1956 is now seen as the decisive starting point of modern British drama, and the policy created a new generation of British playwrights. The first wave included John Osborne, Arnold Wesker, John Arden, Ann Jellicoe, N F Simpson and Edward Bond. Early seasons included new international plays by Bertolt Brecht, Eugène Ionesco, Samuel Beckett, Jean-Paul Sartre and Marguerite Duras.

The theatre started with the 400-seat proscenium arch Theatre Downstairs, and then in 1969 opened a second theatre, the 60-seat studio Theatre Upstairs. Productions in the Theatre Upstairs have transferred to the West End, such as Caryl Churchill's Far Away, Conor McPherson's The Weir, Kevin Elyot's My Night With Reg and Ariel Dorfman's Death and the Maiden. The Royal Court also co-produces plays which have transferred to the West End or toured internationally, such as Sebastian Barry's The Steward of Christendom and Mark Ravenhill's Shopping and Fucking (with Out of Joint), Martin McDonagh's The Beauty Queen Of Leenane (with Druid Theatre Company), Ayub Khan-Din's East is East (with Tamasha Theatre Company, and now a feature film).

Since 1994 the Royal Court's artistic policy has again been vigorously directed to finding and producing a new generation of playwrights. The writers include Joe Penhall, Rebecca Prichard, Michael Wynne, Nick Grosso, Judy Upton, Meredith Oakes, Sarah Kane, Anthony Neilson, Judith Johnson, James Stock, Jez Butterworth, Marina Carr, Simon Block, Martin McDonagh, Mark Ravenhill, Ayub Khan-Din, Tamantha Hammerschlag, Jess Walters, Che Walker, Conor McPherson, Simon Stephens, Richard Bean, Roy

photo: Andy Chopping

Williams, Gary Mitchell, Mick Mahoney, Rebecca Gilman, Christopher Shinn, Kia Corthron, David Gieselmann, Marius von Mayenburg and David Eldridge. This expanded programme of new plays has been made possible through the support of A.S.K Theater Projects, the Jerwood Charitable Foundation, the American Friends of the Royal Court and many in association with the Royal National Theatre Studio.

In recent years there have been record-breaking productions at the box office, with capacity houses for Jez Butterworth's Mojo, Sebastian Barry's The Steward of Christendom, Martin McDonagh's The Beauty Queen of Leenane, Ayub Khan-Din's East is East, Eugène Ionesco's The Chairs, David Hare's My Zinc Bed and Conor McPherson's The Weir, which transferred to the West End in October 1998 and ran for nearly two years at the Duke of York's Theatre.

The newly refurbished theatre in Sloane Square opened in February 2000, with a policy still inspired by the first artistic director George Devine. The Royal Court is an international theatre for new plays and new playwrights, and the work shapes contemporary drama in Britain and overseas.

AWARDS FOR
THE ROYAL COURT

Ariel Dorfman's Death and the Maiden and John Guare's Six Degrees of Separation won the Olivier Award for Best Play in 1992 and 1993 respectively. Terry Johnson's Hysteria won the 1994 Olivier Award for Best Comedy, and also the Writers' Guild Award for Best West End Play. Kevin Elyot's My Night with Reg won the 1994 Writers' Guild Award for Best Fringe Play, the Evening Standard Award for Best Comedy, and the 1994 Olivier Award for Best Comedy. Joe Penhall was joint winner of the 1994 John Whiting Award for Some Voices. Sebastian Barry won the 1995 Writers' Guild Award for Best Fringe Play, the 1995 Critics' Circle Award and the 1997 Christopher Ewart-Biggs Literary Prize for The Steward of Christendom, and the 1995 Lloyds Private Banking Playwright of the Year Award. Jez Butterworth won the 1995 George Devine Award for Most Promising Playwright, the 1995 Writers' Guild New Writer of the Year Award, the Evening Standard Award for Most Promising Playwright and the 1995 Olivier Award for Best Comedy for Mojo. Phyllis Nagy won the 1995 Writers' Guild Award for Best Regional Play for Disappeared.

The Royal Court won the 1995 Prudential Award for Theatre and was the overall winner of the 1995 Prudential Award for the Arts for creativity, excellence, innovation and accessibility. The Royal Court Theatre Upstairs won the 1995 Peter Brook Empty Space Award for innovation and excellence in theatre.

Michael Wynne won the 1996 Meyer-Whitworth Award for The Knocky. Martin McDonagh won the 1996 George Devine Award, the 1996 Writers' Guild Best Fringe Play Award, the 1996 Critics' Circle Award and the 1996 Evening Standard Award for Most Promising Playwright for The Beauty Queen of Leenane. Marina Carr won the 19th Susan Smith Blackburn Prize (1996/7) for Portia Coughlan. Conor McPherson won the 1997 George Devine Award, the 1997 Critics' Circle Award and the 1997 Evening Standard Award for Most Promising Playwright for The Weir. Ayub Khan-Din won the 1997 Writers' Guild Award for Best West End Play, the 1997 Writers' Guild New Writer of the Year Award and the 1996 John Whiting Award for East is East. Anthony Neilson won the 1997 Writers' Guild Award for Best Fringe Play for The Censor.

At the 1998 Tony Awards, Martin McDonagh's The Beauty Queen of Leenane (co-production with Druid Theatre Company) won four awards including Garry Hynes for Best Director and was nominated for a further two. Eugene Ionesco's The Chairs (co-production with Theatre de

Complicite) was nominated for six Tony awards. David Hare won the 1998 Time Out Live Award for Outstanding Achievement and six awards in New York including the Drama League, Drama Desk and New York Critics Circle Award for Via Dolorosa. Sarah Kane won the 1998 Arts Foundation Fellowship in Playwriting. Rebecca Prichard won the 1998 Critics' Circle Award for Most Promising Playwright for Yard Gal.

Conor McPherson won the 1999 Olivier Award for Best New Play for The Weir. The Royal Court won the 1999 ITI Award for Excellence in International Theatre. Sarah Kane's Cleansed was judged Best Foreign Language Play in 1999 by Theater Heute in Germany. Gary Mitchell won the 1999 Pearson Best Play Award for Trust. Rebecca Gilman was joint winner of the 1999 George Devine Award and won the 1999 Evening Standard Award for Most Promising Playwright for The Glory of Living. Roy Williams and Gary Mitchell were joint winners of the George Devine Award 2000 for Most Promising Playwright for Lift Off and The Force of Change respectively. At the Barclays Theatre Awards 2000 presented by the TMA, Richard Wilson won the Best Director Award for David Gieselmann's Mr Kolpert and Jeremy Herbert won the Best Designer Award for Sarah Kane's 4.48 Psychosis. Gary Mitchell won the Evening Standard's Charles Wintour Award 2000 for Most Promising Playwright for The Force of Change. Stephen Jeffreys' I Just Stopped by to See The Man won an AT&T: On Stage Award 2000.

In 1999, the Royal Court won the European theatre prize New Theatrical Realities, presented at Taormina Arte in Sicily, for its efforts in recent years in discovering and producing the work of young British dramatists.

ROYAL COURT BOOKSHOP

The bookshop offers a wide range of playtexts, theatre books, screenplays and art-house videos with over 1,000 titles. Located in the downstairs Bar and Food area, the bookshop is open Monday to Saturday, afternoons and evenings.

Many Royal Court playtexts are available for just £2 including the plays in the current season and recent works by David Hare, Conor McPherson, Martin Crimp, Sarah Kane, David Mamet, Phyllis Nagy, Gary Mitchell, Marina Carr, Martin McDonagh, Ayub Khan-Din, Jim Cartwright and Rebecca Prichard. We offer a 10% reduction to students on a range of titles.
Further information : 020 7565 5024

REBUILDING THE ROYAL COURT

In 1995, the Royal Court was awarded a National Lottery grant through the Arts Council of England, to pay for three quarters of a £26m project to completely rebuild our 100-year old home. The rules of the award required the Royal Court to raise £7.6m in partnership funding. The building has been completed thanks to the generous support of those listed below.

We are particularly grateful for the contributions of over 5,700 audience members.

THE AMERICAN FRIENDS OF THE ROYAL COURT THEATRE

AFRCT support the mission of the Royal Court and are primarily focused on raising funds to enable the theatre to produce new work by emerging American writers. Since this not-for-profit organisation was founded in 1997, AFRCT has contributed to seven productions including Rebecca Gilman's Spinning Into Butter. They have also supported the participation of young artists in the Royal Court's acclaimed International Residency.

If you would like to support the ongoing work of the Royal Court, please contact the Development Department on 020 7565 5050.

Funded by
THE
ARTS
COUNCIL
OF ENGLAND

PROGRAMME SUPPORTERS

The Royal Court (English Stage Company Ltd) receives its principal funding from London Arts. It is also supported financially by a wide range of private companies and public bodies and earns the remainder of its income from the box office and its own trading activities.
The Royal Borough of Kensington & Chelsea gives an annual grant to the Royal Court Young Writers' Programme and the London Boroughs Grants Committee provides project funding for a number of play development initiatives.

Royal Court Registered Charity number 231242.

The Jerwood Charitable Foundation continues to support new plays by new playwrights with the series of Jerwood New Playwrights. Since 1993 the A.S.K. Theater Projects of Los Angeles has funded a Playwrights' Programme at the theatre. Bloomberg Mondays, a continuation of the Royal Court's reduced price ticket scheme, is supported by Bloomberg. Sky has also generously committed to a two-year sponsorship of the Royal Court Young Writers' Festival.

Recently Stage Hands donors, who are members of the Royal Court audience, supported three plays: My Zinc Bed by David Hare, Far Away by Caryl Churchill and I Just Stopped By to See The Man by Stephen Jeffreys.

TRUSTS AND FOUNDATIONS
American Friends of the Royal Court Theatre
Carlton Television Trust
Gerald Chapman Fund
Cultural Foundation Deutsche Bank
The Genesis Foundation
The Goldsmiths Company
Jerwood Charitable Foundation
The John Lyons Charity
Laura Pels Foundation
Quercus Charitable Trust
The Peggy Ramsay Foundation
The Peter Sharp Foundation
Royal Victoria Hall Foundation
The Trusthouse Charitable Foundation

MAJOR SPONSORS
A.S.K. Theater Projects
AT&T
Barclays plc
Bloomberg
Sky
Credit Suisse First Boston
Francis Finlay
Lever Fabergé
(through Arts & Business New Partners)
Royal College of Psychiatrists

BUSINESS MEMBERS
Goldman Sachs International
Laporte plc
Lazard Brothers & Co. Ltd
Elida Fabergé
McCABES
Redwood Publishing
Simons Muirhead & Burton
J Walter Thompson

INDIVIDUAL MEMBERS
Patrons
David H Adams
Advanpress

Katie Bradford
Mrs Alan Campbell-Johnson
Gill Carrick
Chris Corbin
David Day
Greg Dyke
Thomas Fenton
Ralph A Fields
John Flower
Mike Frain
Edna & Peter Goldstein
Judy & Frank Grace
David Graham
Phil Hobbs
Homevale Ltd
JHJ & SF Lewis
Lex Service plc
Barbara Minto
Michael & Mimi Naughton
New Penny Productions Ltd
Martin Newson
AT Poeton & Son Ltd.
André Ptaszynski, Really Useful Theatres
David Rowland
Sir George Russell
Bernard Shapero
Carl & Martha Tack
Mr & Mrs Anthony Weldon
Richard Wilson
George & Moira Yip

Benefactors
Anastasia Alexander
Lesley E Alexander
Batia Asher
Elaine Mitchell Attias
Thomas Bendhem
Jody Berger
Keith & Helen Bolderson
Jeremy Bond
Mr & Mrs F H Bradley III
Mrs Elly Brook JP
Julian Brookstone
Debbi & Richard Burston
Yuen-Wei Chew
Carole & Neville Conrad

Conway Van Gelder
Coppard & Co.
Barry Cox
Curtis Brown Ltd
Deborah Davis
Zöe Dominic
Robyn Durie
Lorraine Esdaile
Winston & Jean Fletcher
Claire & William Frankel
Nicholas Fraser
Robert Freeman
J Garcia
Beverley & Nathaniel Gee
Norman Gerard
Henny Gestetner OBE
Jacqueline & Jonathan Gestetner
Michael Goddard
Carolyn Goldbart
Sally Greene
Byron Grote
Sue & Don Guiney
Hamilton Asper Management
Anna Home CBE
Amanda Howard Associates
ICM Ltd
Trevor Ingman
Lisa Irwin-Burgess
Peter Jones
Paul Kaju & Jane Peterson
Peter & Maria Kellner
Diana King
Clico Kingsbury
Lee & Thompson
CA Leng
Lady Lever
Colette & Peter Levy
Ian Mankin
Christopher Marcus
Nicola McFarland
James McIvor
Mr & Mrs Roderick R McManigal
Mae Modiano
Eva Monley

Joan Moynihan
Georgia Oetker
Paul Oppenheimer
Mr & Mrs Michael Orr
Maria Peacock
Pauline Pinder
Carol Rayman
Angharad Rees
John & Rosemarie Reynolds
John Ritchie
Bernice & Victor Sandelson
John Sandoe (Books) Ltd
Nicholas Selmes
Lois Sieff OBE
Peregrine Simon
David & Patricia Smalley
Brian D Smith
John Soderquist
Max Stafford-Clark
Sue Stapely
Ann Marie Starr
Anthony Wigram

STAGE HANDS CIRCLE
Graham Billing
Andrew Cryer
Lindy Fletcher
Mr R Hopkins
Philip Hughes Trust
Dr A V Jones
Roger Jospe
Miss A Lind-Smith
Mr J Mills
Nevin Charitable Trust
Jeremy Priestley
Ann Scurfield
Brian Smith
Harry Streets
C C Wright

Timberlake Wertenbaker
Credible Witness

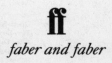

faber and faber

Published in 2001
by Faber and Faber Limited
3 Queen Square, London WC1N 3AU
First published in the United States in 2001 by Faber and Faber Inc.
an affiliate of Farrar, Straus and Giroux LLC, New York

Typeset by Country Setting, Kingsdown, Kent CT14 8ES
Printed in England by Mackays of Chatham plc, Chatham, Kent

A CIP record for this book
is available from the British Library

ISBN 0-571-20937-8

2 4 6 8 10 9 7 5 3 1

For John

Then thus I turn me from my country's light,
To dwell in solemn shades of endless night.

Shakespeare, *Richard II*, I, iii

Characters

in order of appearance

Alexander Karagy
Petra Karagy
Paul
Anna
Ali
Henry
Aziz
Ameena
Shivan
Leon
Simon

PROLOGUE

*A small archaeological dig in Northern Greece. Alexander
Karagy guides a group of children.*

Alexander *Ke tora,* children, tell me this: *pos
anakalyptoume tyn istoria?* How do you find history?
Look at these walls: dug up a few years ago. Before
then, a field of wheat in Northern Greece. Now: five
thousand years of Macedonian history. See here: we
have an Iron Age layer, but above, on exactly the same
alignment, a street from the Bronze Age. A new history
built on top of old histories. Then, a devastating fire.
Later, maybe here, a house belonging to a Macedonian
general, a house where Alexander the Great stayed,
planning the Persian campaign. That house too was
buried and the land criss-crossed by Romans, Byzantines,
Turks collecting taxes, Englishmen planting cotton.
A school was built here to teach Bulgarian, burnt, then
another school to teach Greek. Greeks killed Germans
here, a Communist killed a Royalist cousin. A wedding
group sang, a family danced here before fleeing abroad –
and finally the Greek field of wheat, covering all.

That, children, is your Macedonian history. Not one
layer of Greek wheat, but layer upon layer, all valuable,
because all of it your history.

Now I want you to go into your villages and uncover
the layers. No, not by digging up your cellars – uncover
the bands of your history in the people, in your families.
History always has witnesses. Find them, and if that is
too late, the witnesses of witnesses. A distant memory,
a thread of gossip, a half-remembered language. Go to
your grandmothers who have hoarded memories, kept

words hidden in the folds of their clothes. Go to the old man muttering in the café. Greek? He remembers other languages, suppressed songs, he might even sing one if no one is listening. And his friends will tell you that their great-grandfathers fought with Alexander the Great and that Alexander the Great was always a Macedonian.

Two shadows appear, come nearer.

The layers are well covered, because every generation has thugs who want to bury the past and level the ground. I send you on an uneasy quest, dangerous. But your history lies buried like these walls and, if you lose it you will be poor, and flat. Go now. Run back to your houses, remember my words. Go, quickly! *Grigora, pedia, figete.* Run!

A moment of paralysis. Alexander holds up his arms to avert the blows.

SCENE ONE

Heathrow Airport.
Petra Karagy. Paul.
Petra holds up a photograph of Alexander.

Petra Where is he?

Paul Passport control is this way.

Petra Where?

Paul Go through passport control, pick up your luggage, follow the green arrow through the doors: he'll be waiting for you.

Petra You've seen him?

Paul Heathrow's a busy airport.

Petra You could not miss my son, he is noble-looking, even with the bruises. He looks like Alexander the Great. We are descendants. You know Alexander the Great?

Paul Sikander the Great, Sikandra Bhasha, we have temples to him, he's an Indian God.

Petra Alexander the Great was Macedonian. He conquered India. What have you done with my son?

Paul Is this your passport? (*He studies it.*)

Petra It's good, no?

Paul Amateurs. You'll have to come with me.

Petra I want to see my son.

Paul It's against the rules to say this, but I'm a kind man and you look tired.

Petra I am tired of waiting for my son. Where is he?

Paul Listen carefully: when the officer looks at your passport and tells you it's not valid, tell him you are seeking political asylum.

Petra I do not want an asylum. I am looking for my son.

Paul If you don't do it now, you'll be in trouble later. Repeat after me: I am claiming –

Petra I do not need to be taught English words. My great-grandfather was English. When he came to Macedonia, he was received, lavish hospitality was proffered. He left a child and a pride. We have always spoken English. My son is best. I sent him here to be received, but I have heard nothing. Do you recognise him?

Paul I see thousands come through, looking like that, from places I've never even heard of.

Petra Ma-ce-do-nia.

Paul You can explain it all to the immigration officials.

Petra Everyone knows about Macedonia.

Paul This job is one big geography lesson: every day
I hear of a new country. Please don't make trouble: come
with me.

Petra You have disappeared my son and now you try to
disappear my country. I do not believe you do not know
Macedonia. I am looking for my son Alexander of
Macedonia and I do not move until you produce him
before me.

SCENE TWO

*A dilapidated community centre in England. Alexander,
Ali, Henry and Anna.*

Alexander What is an exile, children?

The children do not answer.

An exile has lost his house, her village, his country and
cannot go back home. An exile is a guest in a new
country.

Ali and Anna snigger.

We are guests in England.

Henry spits.

An exile learns to love and respect his new country.

More sniggers.

But this will not happen until the exile has lamented his
loss, her grief, that grim accident of history that chased
him out.

Anna jumps up.

Anna will say it was her neighbours, she knows who they are and she wants revenge, yes, but let us first learn to lament.

> *The children begin to giggle. Alexander ignores this and they gradually subside.*

Today, we will cry for Ali, even though his name is not Ali. Ali has forgotten his name. He came to England two years ago with the name Michel Jeune. That wasn't his name but he'd been told to learn this new name because it is easier to get into England with a French name than an Algerian one. When it became clear Michel Jeune didn't even speak French he was put in a detention centre and there he was called Gene because no one could pronounce Jeune. He was only fourteen so he was sent to a hostel where they called him John and then to school where someone decided he was Michael Young. Now Ali answers to any name, Mike, John, Nigel, Young, Old, Hey, You. We call him Ali because at least Ali is an Algerian name.

One day Ali will remember his name. And with his name he will remember his home, his friends, the food he liked, the smells of his village, the good times, because history is also the good times.

> *Anna and Henry hold their noses, but Ali is very still.*

Ali will remember his name, but until then we will cry for him, his lost self, we will cry for Ali. We cry for Ali.

> *Alexander intones the name, both Henry and Anna get into this.*

Anna Ali.

Alexander/Anna Ali.

Henry Ali.

Alexander turns quickly to Henry.

Alexander Henry does remember his name, but he won't tell it to us. Henry's name is all he has left and he is afraid that if he loses that too, he will no longer exist. So we call him Henry.

Henry remembers his country, Eritrea. He remembers his school. Henry remembers one day at school, he cannot forget that day, he tells us about it again and again and now we are going to lament that day.

It was late afternoon, it was hot.

The children have done this before, they go for it.

Anna Very hot.

Alexander There had been trouble in the town.

Ali There is trouble every night.

Alexander As he started walking home from school, Henry saw four men. He thought of running away.

Ali There's nowhere to run.

Anna The men walk down the road with him.

Alexander No one says a word.

Ali Henry whistles to show he isn't afraid.

The children all whistle.

Anna The men smile.

Henry They walk me round the corner to my house. (*He looks.*)

Anna On the front of the house.

Henry From the low roof.

The children stop, hesitate.

Alexander Hang four bodies, naked, mutilated. The body of Henry's father.

Anna Henry's mother.

Ali Henry's older brother.

Henry (*looking*) Uncle!

Alexander The men speak for the first time.

Ali 'That's your punishment.'

Anna/Ali 'That's your punishment.'

Alexander They say.

Anna They walk away.

Alexander Henry doesn't know what he did to deserve such a punishment. Now Henry is afraid to do anything in case he gets punished again. Whenever Henry starts a drawing, a game, he hears the men say:

Ali 'That's your punishment.'

Alexander And he stops.

Henry 'That's your punishment. That's your punishment.'

Alexander These words have paralysed Henry like the venom of a poisonous snake. We'll cry for Henry, for the frozen memory, and maybe one day the poison of those words will ooze out, the wound heal, and Henry will tell us his secret name.

Ali cries. Henry is very still. Alexander moves quickly to Anna.

Alexander Anna.

Anna No one cries for Anna!

Alexander No one cries for Anna and no one laughs at Anna.

When Anna hears someone laugh, she gets very angry, she kicks, she bites, she throws things. Anna is very strong. Anna speaks beautiful English, she is good in maths. When she came here two years ago, the teachers said she was a wonderful girl. Now they say she's bad. She doesn't listen. I think Anna doesn't listen because she is afraid she will hear the laughter of the men who came for her mother.

Anna clenches her fists. Alexander sees this.

Anna wants to be the only one who laughs. Catch a little girl, sit on top of her, hear her beg for mercy, then laugh. Knock down a small boy. Anna comes from an inflamed part of Europe where laughter belongs to the strong who sit on top of history. We will not cry for Anna, but we will cry for her country where screams for mercy dripped down the walls, but the neighbours laughed, we will cry for her mother who didn't have time to cry for herself, we will cry, and maybe instead of hitting us, Anna will take pity on us and dry our tears.

Alexander leans his face close to Anna. She clenches her fists, raises them, unclenches them and moves her hand to his face.

SCENE THREE

Barbed wire. A gray space.
Several figures huddled over themselves, isolated.
It could be a refugee camp anywhere in the world, but in fact, it is a detention centre in England.
Petra, Aziz, Ameena, Leon and Shivan.
Petra holds up photographs. Nothing happens. She moves to Aziz, shows him the photos.

Petra You have seen him?

Aziz, very spaced out, looks, nods.

Yes? You have seen him!

Aziz I have seen him?

Petra Maybe he has a beard now.

Aziz looks. Nods.

Aziz More handsome with a beard.

Petra thrusts another photograph.

Petra This is older, but close up.

Aziz pushes it away.

Aziz Please: never the head not attached.

Petra Maybe he's thinner now.

Aziz Hungry.

Petra You've seen him then? Alexander.

Aziz Alexander . . .

Petra Like Alexander the Great.

Aziz Al Skender al Adeen. Alexandria. I know
Alexander the Great.

Petra Where is he?

Aziz Alexander the Great? You're looking for Alexander
the Great?

Petra My son!

Aziz Alexander the Great is your son? Ah. (*He nods.
Then nods off.*)

Petra You don't look well. Are you eating enough fruit?

Aziz laughs.

Aziz *Les oranges. Les oranges d'Alger. Je les mangerais . . .*
If only I will keep my head.

Petra gives up, goes to Ameena.

Petra Women have better memories for faces.

Petra shows her the photos. Ameena shudders.

Please . . . you have seen him?

Ameena starts shaking.

A young man, handsome too.

Ameena (*shaking*) Sorry. Sorry. Sorry.

Ameena rocks herself. Her clothes fall loose from her shoulders. Petra covers them.

Petra You should not behave like that in front of men. It is not seemly.

Aziz laughs.

Ameena Sorry. Sorry . . .

She starts crying. Tries to take Petra's hand. Petra moves away, goes to Leon.
Leon is carving a flute. He does not shift concentration. Petra sees this and gives up. She goes to Shivan, who is reading. She waits.

Petra I always let my son finish the page.

Shivan closes the book.

Shivan Milton.

Petra English.

Shivan Very.

Petra That's good.

Shivan My name is Shivan, Shivan Rajagopal. (*Shivan holds out his hand for the photographs. He studies them carefully.*) Sensitive. Even passionate. An artist? No. Actor? I have it: a teacher.

Petra You've seen him!

Shivan I'm good at faces.

Petra He came to Heathrow. They said if I came here, they would help me find him.

Shivan They said that.

Petra Do you know what happened to my son?

Shivan I can guess.

Petra You do not need to fear to say anything to a descendant of Macedonian warriors. (*Pause.*) He was killed at Heathrow . . .?

Shivan This is England.

Petra I know about England and its ancient Parliament, but my son has disappeared. He had enemies. What happened at Heathrow?

Shivan Same as me. He will have been questioned.

Petra Questioned? Tortured?

Shivan Not physically, no.
  Then he was probably sent to a hostel.

Petra A hospital?

Shivan A B-and-B. A hotel.

Petra That is hospitality. More like England. I hope it is clean. Where is it?

Shivan There are many all over the country.

Petra I will go to the hotels. I will search every street of every village and town and ask. In the civil war, Mr Raja –

Shivan Doctor Rajagopal . . . Shivan.

Petra I walked twenty kilometres every night to feed my uncles. They hid in the marshes and I walked in mud and water to leave no footprints. I still know how to walk. Which is the way out?

Shivan Mrs – Mrs –

Petra Karagy. Petra Karagy.

Shivan Mrs Karagy, it's night time.

Petra I walked at night to my uncles, through the reeds. I always found them.

Shivan The doors are locked.

Petra Where is the person with the keys?

Shivan Mrs Karagy, may I explain –

Petra Olla, eh – olla! Open the doors.

Shivan Mrs Karagy, no one will come.

Petra Olla! Open up!

Shivan Mrs Karagy, we are locked in.

Petra Locked. Why?

Shivan Did you ask for asylum at Heathrow?

Petra The guard said I must. He tricked me. They want to keep me in an asylum – I am not mad, Dr Rajagopal!

Shivan No, Mrs Karagy, you are not mad. And this is not an asylum.

Petra Have they locked me in prison then? Is my son here too?

Shivan This is not a prison, but you are locked up, Mrs Karagy, you are in a British detention centre.

Aziz laughs. Leon concentrates.

Ameena Sorry. Sorry . . .

SCENE FOUR

Alexander. The children. A silence, then slowly:

Alexander Life to death, peace to war, home to exile. In my country, we sing, but we often also dance the grief of loss. Today, we will lament a name, the name Alexander Karagy.

It was a name given to a child in baptism in a village that was then in Yugoslavia but is now in a country the Greeks refuse to call Macedonia. The child grew up in another village, in an area which is now the very north of Greece, but is also called Macedonia. The child became a teacher who himself respected the emotive force of names, the way history reverberates in a few letters, and he spent many years teaching the meaning of that complex, bitterly fought-over name: Macedonia. But some people in his country didn't like this, shadows fell across his path, and the teacher was forced to flee to England, which he could only do by borrowing a stranger's name. He believed it would not take him long to get his true name back. While waiting for his papers, he has worked with you, trying to help you find your own names. He has loved this work.

But today, your teacher has been told the name Alexander Karagy does not exist, never existed. It seems the name is in no records, nowhere – and there will be no papers giving your teacher back the name Alexander Karagy. And because you can't have a no-name – an impostor – teaching vulnerable children, he has been told – very politely – he has until five o'clock this afternoon to leave. I can't ask you to cry for your teacher, because how can you cry for nobody from nowhere? But we can lament the dying of a name. The name Alexander Karagy will now dance out of this room into silence and disappear. So let us cry for the name Alexander Karagy. We cry

for the name Alexander Karagy – Alexander Karagy.
Alexander Karagy. Alexander Karagy.

*Alexander slowly dances himself out of the room. The
children giggle, then wait, astonished, then leave.*

SCENE FIVE

*The detention centre, some weeks later. Simon Le Britten,
Petra Karagy, and Leon, carving.*

Simon We have no record of an Alexander Karagy
entering this country.

Petra He fled to England for protection.

Simon If he had applied for political asylum, he would
be on our files.

Petra Maybe a different name.

Simon What name?

Petra I refused to learn it. I sold two of my best fields of
wheat and my great-grandmother's English necklace and
they couldn't even give him his right name. What do you
expect? They're Albanians.

Simon Who?

Petra He had to use a name already there, only change
the picture. All this money and they couldn't even give
him his name.

Simon You're telling me you bought a false passport for
your son.

Petra When they beat him, they took his identity card.

Simon Who beat him?

Petra If I knew I would kill them.

Simon Why would 'they' do this?

Petra History.

Simon Did your son have a history of drugs?

Petra He had a history of history, the history he taught.

Simon There are a lot of drugs moving through that part of Greece, Mrs Karagy.

Petra We call it Macedonia, Mr England.

Simon Le Britten. Your village is Greek.

Petra It is now inside the Greek border, its history is Macedonian, that is what my son was teaching. They didn't like it.

Simon The mysterious men?

Petra People in the village and the other villages too. My son could have taught in a big city. He chose to come back to the village, to the children. My son is possessed by history, Mr Britain, he searches out its truth the way a young husband explores his wife's body. My father died fighting the Germans just before I was born, and his father was a fighter but Alexander is a lover, not a warrior. It's Alexander the Great's intelligence he inherited. And stubbornness. They would have killed him.

Simon For teaching in a village school? Greece is a democracy, it's part of the EU.

Petra In Greece you cannot teach unless you swear allegiance. Some people were whispering he was not a patriot.

Simon If he was beaten, he could have gone to the police.

Petra He believed it was the police who beat him up.

Simon For teaching history!

Petra Do you know Greece?

Simon Mrs Karagy, I have been in this job for eight years. You wouldn't believe the stories I hear. The challenge of this job is to find the truth of a story and it's a challenge I relish. I'm like a historian myself, sifting the evidence. Now I'll tell you the facts of this case.

Petra You know them!

Simon Your son was in trouble over drugs. You would be last to know.

Petra I knew even my son's dreams.

Simon Whether your son was in trouble with the police or a gang, I don't know. But he knew that when he came here, he wouldn't get away with claiming political asylum for long – assuming he did that under his false name – and so he did what other illegal immigrants of his ilk do, he slipped quietly through the net. He vanished, like some twenty thousand – maybe forty, even fifty thousand now – other illegal entries into this country. They have no records, no papers, they find sustenance in their communities, we only catch up with them when they die or get caught in a raid. Until then, they are invisible, disappeared.

Petra I said he had been disappeared. I want you to find him!

Simon Many young men become pimps. I have listened to you and observed you, Mrs Karagy, I am convinced you are an honest woman, that's why I'm taking so much trouble – look at all these cases.

My advice to you is to go quietly back to your village and one day your son will come back to you, probably in a Mercedes, smoking a cigar, some tart on his arm –

Petra You are dishonouring my name, in my country that could get you killed!

Simon Fortunately, we are in England. I believe your son is dishonouring himself.

Petra You think because I am an old woman you can confuse me? We are not gypsy beggars, we own land. A pimp! My son who caressed books as a child.

Simon Maybe he only wanted to better himself. I can put myself in his place. When I was his age, I wanted to emigrate to Australia, but they wanted builders not people with management skills.

Petra Many people from our villages emigrated to Australia.

Simon There you are, they were accepted, I wasn't. The difference between me and your son is that I accepted the situation. I didn't try to cheat my way in.

Petra My son never cheated. The mayor's son tried to buy his marks.

Simon He came to this country with a false passport.

Petra What else could he do?

Simon You love your son, you defend him. I admire you for that, but you're going to be disappointed in him. I have a hunch he's disappointed in himself. You say he hasn't been in touch for three years. Why? Immigrants come here thinking life will be easy. It's hard enough for us. I was a middle manager in the Post Office. I loved my job. There were redundancies. I was very bitter at first, but I'm glad to have this job at my age. I don't need to tell a woman of your experience that life is full of grey.

Petra Grey? When my mother came out of the camps in 1950, she didn't talk, she only painted. She gave me a painting of a flag: red, white and black. She called it the flag of history and labelled red for blood, black for grief, white for hope.

I measured the colours. They were all the same. Except white looks bigger.

Simon smiles.

Simon Hope, yes, I understand.

Pause.

I don't often get a chance to talk like this. Your English is excellent.

Pause.

I'll arrange a flight home for you next week. I wish I could do more.

Petra Mr Great Britain.

Simon Le Britten – it's a Norman name, I believe: from *Le Breton.*

Petra rummages in her clothes. She takes out a small bag from which she takes out a rolled handkerchief which she unfolds carefully. She hands a small coin to Simon.

Petra The head of Alexander. Very antique. Gold.

Simon looks at it. Hands it back.

Simon It's beautiful.

Petra For you. To keep.
I wait until you bring me my son.

Simon We don't take bribes in England, Mrs Karagy.

Petra It is a gift. It is not even an obligation. My pleasure.

Simon hands back the coin.

Simon I can't help you further. I have other cases to deal with. (*He turns to go.*)

Petra Mr Le Britten – my great-grandmother was from a North Macedonian village where they spoke Bulgarian. She married a Greek from Asia Minor who had a mill in Assiros. Her sister married his brother. Bulgarian women were beautiful and the Greek men rich. After the wedding feasts, my great-grandmother and great-aunt rode with the two bridegrooms to Assiros. The villagers gathered in the market place to greet them. It's a big market place, it's always been a wealthy village. The couples dismounted and the bridegrooms asked the two women to salute the mill which would shower their children with riches. This they did. Then the bridegrooms asked the women to kneel and swear never to speak Bulgarian again because now they were Greeks and their children would be Greek. My great-grandmother's sister knelt. My great-grandmother, even though she was only sixteen, remained standing and shook her head.

Her husband asked her again, slowly. She shook her head again. He hit her. The villagers murmured approval, she was humiliating him in public. He beat her more. She still refused to kneel. From that day, we became known as the women who refuse to kneel. Because we still speak Bulgarian and we never kneel to anything or to anyone, except to God and sometimes not even that. Mr Le Britten, I come from the family of the women who refuse to kneel. Look: I am getting down on my knees – in front of you – let Alexander the Great and my great-grandmother and my mother forgive me, I beg you, I clasp your knees to bring me back my son.

SCENE SIX

The street. Alexander, Henry.

   Alexander sweeps the pavement. Henry comes with various imaginary weapons and their corresponding sounds. Henry starts by aiming a sniper rifle at Alexander then recognises him.

Alexander Henry.

Henry Teacher!

   Alexander shakes his head, shows his broom and orange overcoat.

Henry (*nodding*) Minesweeper. (*Henry points to himself.*) Freedom fighter. (*He takes a few grenades and throws them. He now holds a Kalashnikov – imaginary.*) Look at that one on his knees. Coward! (*Henry shoots.*) That's your punishment.

   I kill all.

Alexander And then?

Henry All dead!

Alexander Who'll be left to run the village?

Henry Me! (*He dances over imaginary corpses.*)

Alexander Tell me about your village, Henry.

Henry My village is big. When you want to go somewhere and there's a house in front of you, you walk through the house. If someone is cooking, they feed you, if they are talking, they talk with you, or maybe they offer you water.

   Here, even in the street, no one talks to you, no one opens their doors, no one gives you water. Here, everything is locked.

I kicked this boy today. Headmaster said I do it again he throws me out of school for good.

Alexander Why not try to make a life here?

Henry Rubbish-dump place.

Alexander Think of yourself as a very important guest. You wouldn't insult a house that welcomed you.

Henry They don't Welcome here.

Alexander Maybe they express it differently.

Henry Like: get out! Filthy bogey scum.

> *Alexander bends on himself. Henry studies him for a moment, offers him a packet of crisps.*

Henry Teacher?

Alexander Eat them yourself, Henry.
Maybe you can find one thing you like here, and like that one thing a lot.

Henry One thing.
Maybe one day I tell you my name.

Alexander I'd like that very much.

Henry But then you have to come over to my side.

Alexander I am on your side.

Henry Then why you sweep my mines away?

Alexander Mines are bad for all sides.

Henry Are you fighting for your country?

> *Alexander doesn't answer.*

Then you know nothing.

Alexander One thing you like.

Henry turns to go. Alexander starts sweeping.

Henry Careful over there. The mines are very hidden.

Henry picks his way out. Alexander stares out in hunger and solitude.

SCENE SEVEN

The detention centre. Ameena, Shivan, Aziz, Leon and Petra sit in the grey light of morning. Only Shivan is reading. Paul comes on.

Paul Good morning, ladies and gentlemen. Time for your pills. No cheating, no hoarding, no trading.

He gives pills to Leon and Ameena, who swallow them silently. He goes to Aziz.

Paul And two for you.

Aziz Doctor said four.

Paul He writes two here.

Aziz I need four. I'm going crazy!

Paul Ask the doctor next time.

Aziz Next week! I'm going crazy today.

Paul I'm not a doctor.

Aziz (*pointing to Shivan*) Ask him.

Shivan (*looking up from his book*) I am a doctor . . .

Paul ignores this and goes over to Petra.

Paul Four for you.

Shivan That's too many.

Aziz They're mine. Doctor got mixed up.

Paul He writes for the Greek woman. Are you the Greek woman?

Aziz The government said I was a woman for not joining the army to fight the Islamists and they will shoot me. The Islamists said if I didn't join them I was no better than a woman and they will rip my balls out. Other Islamists said the first Islamists were not real Islamists but were working for the government: we were old women for believing them and they'll slit our throats if we don't join them in the mountains. How do you know I'm not a woman? Give me those pills.

Petra I'm not The Greek Woman. He can have them.

Paul I'm trying to help, the doc says you need them badly.

Shivan The doctor saw her for five minutes. He didn't even check her heart.

Paul I do what the doctor says.

Shivan I am a doctor.

Paul At Heathrow I had three different people tell me they were deposed emperors.

Shivan Are you doubting I am a doctor?

Paul I was moved here because I believed too many stories.

Shivan I was a consultant in Sri Lanka.

Paul (*to Petra*) Take them, they make your head feel better.

Petra I don't have a headache.

Shivan The guard we had before believed me.

Paul They make your head happy.

Petra How can my head be happy when my eyes don't find my son?

Shivan I am a doctor.

Aziz (*over*) I keep seeing my head somewhere. Sometimes, it's on the side of the road, looking up at me. Then in my mother's lap and there's blood dripping down her arms. Afterwards, on a balcony, all by itself, and the eyes blink in the sunset. Yesterday I dream they send me back to Algeria and there's my head rolling down the airplane steps, bump, bump, bump.

Paul (*to Petra*) Come on, love, please take them.

Aziz (*speedy*) When I came here I told them I was running away because my head was going to be torn off. We don't accept fear of the future, they tell me, only what happened: were you officially threatened? Officially? There's a civil war on, I say. It' s not officially a civil war, they say. If I don't have more pills my head will come off: officially.

Petra Give him the pills to keep him quiet.

Aziz You're the one always talking about history, old woman. You think you're the only one with history? My grandmother died planting a bomb against the French. But in Algiers, we still learn French. I can't even speak good Arabic. I like American. We watch American movies in secret. The Wild West, that's good history. Algerian history is making my head come off. French history says it's my grandmother's fault and English history says Algerian history doesn't exist. I need pills to keep my head straight.

Petra (*to Paul*) Give me those pills.

Shivan The guard before you took my advice.

Paul (*to Petra*) I have to watch you swallow them.

Petra You're doubting the word of a Macedonian?

Shivan You're doubting my word I'm a doctor!

Aziz You doubt I'm crazy!

Paul Please, all of you, don't make trouble or I'll have to report you.

Shivan I only ask that you believe I am a doctor.

Paul I've been told to watch for any trouble before it's too late. It's because of those troublemakers we had up North. First they rioted, then they went on a hunger strike. They were sent to prison but it was too late for one of them, and now there's this fuss in the newspapers. I saw the photo, I haven't seen a face so thin since my childhood.

Petra Who is so thin – where is the picture? What did he look like?

Paul It's not your son, he was from somewhere else. Imagine starving yourself to death to get what you want. What kind of behaviour is that for a foreigner? It's not as if you're English or even Irish, with rights and things. You're not even supposed to be here. You can't refuse to eat perfectly decent food which is costing the taxpayer all this money, especially when you were probably starving in your own country.

Shivan I am here because I am a doctor.

Petra Did they get what they wanted, the hunger strikers?

Paul They got a lot of attention and our security group was blamed. You know, when we came over, and we were invited after all, we never behaved like that. We did everything to fit in. We worked hard, we kept our heads down, we put up with a lot. I can't make my son understand that, he's always in trouble, but he says he's British.

33

Petra No one can force you to eat?

Paul They can only force-feed you in prison. We had a Jamaican woman who said she'd go on hunger strike but she kept eating sweets. She was a big woman, it took three of us to get her on the plane, she was throwing her head about, she almost started a riot. That's what I mean, you come here and start riots and it makes us all look bad.

Aziz Sometimes I see my head outside there, looking through the wire. The wire's red with blood. I'm going to start a riot if I don't get my pills. (*Aziz starts banging.*)

Paul Quiet! (*to Petra*) I talk too much. Wearing a uniform is a lonely business.

Shivan There have been ten different guards in the months I've been here and they all believed me. They took my advice. Why don't you believe me?

Aziz, banging more loudly, is joined rhythmically by Leon.

Paul Quiet, I said. What's wrong with you people that if someone is friendly you take advantage?

Shivan What kind of a doctor comes to this centre? In another country, he would be measuring the pain threshold of torture victims. Here, he keeps us as quiet as he can without killing us. He doesn't even do that very well.

Aziz gets wilder, moves towards Ameena.

Aziz If I would keep my head on, I will kiss a girl. I need pills to keep my head on.

Ameena trembles, cowers.

Paul Stop that now!

Leon and Aziz start a more frantic beat.

Shivan (*to Paul*) I have been patient for months, polite. I remind myself I can help people anywhere. I am reading *Paradise Lost* for the third time to help endure the humiliation and also to share the power of this language.

Aziz moves back to Ameena.

Aziz If I knew my head doesn't fall off, I dance with a beautiful girl.

Ameena begins to sob.

Paul (*to Aziz*) Leave her alone!

Shivan If we don't share the truth of language, what then? You don't believe I'm a doctor, why should I believe you're a guard? If language disintegrates, there's nothing left. He needs help, you deny him, he riots. You deny me. I know why you deny me. You think, yes, Sri Lanka, that's a Tamil. You look at me with your North Indian superiority and you don't listen. If I'm not Doctor Rajagopal, who am I? Wherefore this forbearance? You won't let me be doctor in this hell? Very well: then shall I be Lucifer, rebel, rioter.

Shivan begins to clap rhythmically. And declaims:

Hail horrors, hail
Infernal world and thou profoundest hell
Receive thy new possessor –

Paul Stop it, all of you. (*to Petra*) I'm going to lose this job too. I'm the one who helped you at the airport, that's why they sent me here, they say I'm not good at authority. If I have to call out there for help, they'll get rid of me.

Shivan
No light, but rather darkness visible
Served only to discover sights of woe,
Regions of sorrow, doleful shades, where peace
And rest can never dwell, hope never come –

*Aziz and Leon try to get Ameena to dance by taking
her hands and forcing her up. She begins to scream
hysterically.*

Ameena No! No! No! No! No!

Paul Stop!

Aziz She screams because she sees the blood from my
neck! it's dripping!

Shivan
Our prison strong, this huge convex of fire
Outrageous to devour, immures us round
And gates of burning adamant . . .
Prohibit all egress.

Ameena No! No! No!

Ameena begins to gasp and yelp.
  *Shivan stops and goes over to her, but doesn't touch
her. Paul tries to hold her.*

Shivan Not a man. Mrs Karagy, quick, hold her! Only
you.

Petra What's wrong with her?

Shivan You're a woman! Can't you see! Help her!

Petra stares at Ameena.

Petra Oh, child. (*She quickly moves to hold her.*)

Paul (*to Shivan*) I have pills for you, too.

*Shivan knocks them out of Paul's hands. Aziz goes on
the floor to collect them. Ameena screams.*

Paul Help! Riot! Riot!

Petra Stop! All of you! Ameena . . .

Ameena subsides. Sobs continuously.

We can't behave like this, it is not dignified.

Nobody needs to riot here because I have decided.

I will bring back my son. I will make visible the disappeared, not just him, you – you. Paul has told me how to do it: as of now, I, Petra Karagy of Macedon, I am going to hunger strike. To the death or to the appearance of my son. Great Alexander, I call on you now to stand by me, help me, and let me remember who I am.

She folds her arms, sits. The others go still. A long moment.

SCENE EIGHT

Alexander, Anna, Ali. Alexander is handing out leaflets. Anna takes one and recognises Alexander.

Anna (*with reproach*) 'Highlights, lowlights, cut, blow dry – manicure included – all products organic –'

Alexander You have to be English to sell *The Big Issue*.

Anna Listen to this: William the Conqueror – 1066 to 1087; William Two, also known as Rufus – 1087 to 1100; Henry One – 1100 to 1135; Stephen – 1135 to 1154; Henry Two – 1154 to 1189; Richard One, the Lion Hearted – I like him – 1189 to 1199: I know them better than anyone.

Alexander Why?

Anna It's English history.

Alexander What about your own history?

Anna (*spits*) Ask me anything about the Tudors.

Alexander Why aren't you in school?

Anna I threw a chair across the classroom. But they think my exam results will be astonishing. John – 1199 to 1216; Henry Three – 1216 to 1272 –

Alexander Don't forget your own history, Anna: have the courage to be complicated.

Anna You're not my teacher!

Alexander I should be.

Anna You walked out. We thought we'd done something.

Alexander I explained I'd lost my name. Didn't you understand?

Anna We never understood anything you said, did we, Ali? But we liked you. We believed you liked us.

Alexander Anna, Ali, I do like you.

Anna Then why did you desert us? Why are you handing out rubbish hairdressing leaflets! (*She crumples the leaflets and throws them in his face.*)

SCENE NINE

The detention centre. Petra, Simon. It is a private conversation in a public space. Shivan is reading, Leon carving.

Simon We have traced your son.

Petra Where is he?

Simon He did not claim asylum at Heathrow, only later – that always makes me suspicious. He worked with

refugee children in one of those dramarama self-
expression type groups they so love in North London,
but he was asked to leave when Greece denied all
knowledge of him.

Petra Greece denied Alexander?

Simon They have no record of his birth.

Petra His father wanted him to have a Slav name as well
as Alexander. The Greek priest wouldn't baptise children
with Slav names. We went to his mother's village across
the border.

Simon You said he was born in Greece.

Petra The birth is recorded by the Church. Try
Yugoslavia.

Simon That is impossible now, Mrs Karagy.

Petra My son was in the university in Thessalonica. You
have to have the best marks to get in.

Simon The university has never heard of him.

Petra That is not possible.

   Pause.

My son said the university had never heard Alexander
the Great was a Macedonian. The administration is
appointed by the government. Some of them are from
the military.

Simon When your son was told he would have to leave
Britain, he vanished, as I suspected. Someone of his
description was cleaning the streets –

Petra My son is an intellectual. He does not know how
to clean!

Simon We have postmen who don't know how to read.
There's a thriving black economy in this country, Mrs

Karagy, It makes me so angry – all these people cheating. I'm determined to find your son, even if I have to look for him myself: I came to tell you to stop your hunger strike.

Petra I stop when you produce his body.

Simon I had a call from a newspaper today, they're on your scent, they'll soon give tongue, that's a hunting term, I took up riding when I worked for the Post Office. If this gets out, we'll get it both ways: we'll be accused of cruelty and we'll be accused of incompetence, we're always caught in the middle. I'm trying to do a decent job, can't you understand that?

Petra Let me look for my son myself.

Simon How would you find him?

Petra I'm a mother, I would smell him.

Simon It's a big city out there.

Petra I have been to Athens.

Simon I can't let you officially into this country. We're already an overpopulated island. Everybody wants to come in. There are twenty million displaced people in Russia alone. And then the gypsies, the Columbians, Asians, all pressing against our doors, hiding in the wheels of airplanes. The newspapers write heartrending stories because they arrive dead of exposure, but we have to bury them. Do you know how much that costs? We had two children from the Congo who died in the hold of a cargo plane, there was such a fuss we had to send the bodies back with the equivalent of a guard of honour. And they learn fast. Last month a man parachuted into a pack of hounds in Dorset. They thought it was a hunt saboteur and attacked him. Now he has a lawyer claiming damages. Even if we took only

40

the genuine victims of torture, Britain would groan under the weight. I'm afraid to turn on the news because every time one of those countries erupts on television, thousands more files pile on my desk. I'm short-staffed, we have antiquated office equipment, but still I do not send people back to be killed and tortured. I feel sorry for those going back to hunger and disease, believe me, but I have to see the marks of torture before I let anyone in. Genuine. Deep. Or the real fear of death. It's easier than you think. There were no torture marks on your son.

Petra He was beaten.

Simon Bar-room brawl.

Petra There is only one bar in our village, I own it.

Simon Young men will fight. Maybe a girl.

Petra He told me he was beaten by the police.

Simon He lied.

Petra gets up and slaps Simon.

Petra No one calls my son a liar.

A pause. Leon and Shivan stare for a moment and then concentrate intently on what they are doing.

Petra What have I done? Alexander killed his favourite Macedonian general in a fit of wrath. Then he cried for days.
I am an old woman. I have not eaten for ten days. I love my son. And I have such pride for him. Your mother would understand.
She would be the same if you disappeared. She would seek you with this cold fear in her stomach. Is she alive, your mother?
She is not alive? I am sorry.

Simon She is alive – but she would not understand.

Petra A mother's heart shivers day and night . . . Ask her . . .

Simon I went away to school, to a boarding school – do you understand?

Petra nods.

A minor public school.

When I was fourteen, I was accused of stealing the housemaster's money box. I hadn't, but two boys said they'd seen me. And my marks weren't that good. I was expelled.

When my mother came to get me, she listened to the housemaster in silence. She took me home in silence. She let me go to bed in silence.

Your son does not deserve you as his mother, Mrs Karagy. I would have been a different man if my mother had slapped that housemaster.

SCENE TEN

Same as before. Leon has finished his flute and starts playing. Aziz joins in, singing, drumming on chairs. The music is jazzy, Afro-Algerian Rai. The singing is for Petra and Ameena, who holds herself next to Petra but can't help drumming the beat. Paul comes on.

Paul There's someone who says he knows your son. (*He listens to the music for a moment.*) You're not supposed to play in here. (*He listens.*) Not bad. Try this. (*He claps a rhythmic variation. Stops himself. To Petra*) We're only supposed to allow close relatives, so be quick. (*to the musicians*) Don't make too much noise or people will think you're having a good time. I'll lose my job.

Why am I so nice?

Alexander comes in. All stare at him and then file out.
    *Petra devours Alexander with her eyes, but doesn't
    move.*

Alexander Mamou.

  Silence

Alexander *Ti kaneis, Mamou.*

Petra Speak in English.

Alexander Mamou, it's me. Alexander.

  Petra looks intently.

Your son. (*He laughs.*) Descendant of Alexander the
Great.
    Mamou –

Petra Take off your shirt.

Alexander Mamou!

Petra I'm not afraid.
    Take off your shirt.

  Alexander does so reluctantly.

Turn around.

Alexander What are you looking for, Mamou?

Petra Let me see your legs.

Alexander That's enough, Mamou, it's me.

Petra And here? (*She points to her crotch.*) Did they do
anything – there?

Alexander I haven't been tortured, Mamou!
    I read about you in the newspapers.

Petra They're threatening you?

Alexander You must stop this hunger strike.

Petra Three years.

Silence.

One thousand and one hundred nights.

Alexander You told me not to write.

Petra I told you not to write the first six months. I was afraid they would follow your trail. After – I told you to write to the name Xenia Xenakis, *Poste Restante*, Athens. You forgot the name.

Alexander slowly shakes his head.

The first time, I took five different buses to Athens in case I was followed. I waited in line hours in the heat with German and American students. The man looked at me strangely, no honest Greek gets letters *poste restante*. There was nothing for Xenia Xenakis. I went back six months later, only two buses this time. Six months again. Last time, I took the airplane.

Every time I saw a tourist in the village I thought maybe you'd sent a message. I gave a lot of English people coffee and water. What did they do to you?

Alexander Nothing.

Petra *Tipota.*

Alexander Nothing. Nothing. Nothing. You wouldn't understand.

Petra I have always understood my son.

Alexander I could have written in the first six months. I taught children, you would have been proud of me. I helped them lament.

Petra Lamenting is for women.

Alexander You must eat, Mamou.

Petra What happened?

Alexander They didn't believe me. They called in someone from the Greek Embassy. He was my age, he was wearing a suit. He told the official my Greek wasn't very good and I was probably Albanian.

Petra The Karagys, Albanians!

Alexander I had only the false passport. I'd pretended I didn't know any English because I was nervous and I thought an interpreter would help. That was two lies – you'd told me the English don't forgive lies. The embassy man misinterpreted everything I said to the official. It made me unsure, hearing it in another language, but so different – I became confused. They didn't want to believe I was beaten by the police, they asked how many, details. I couldn't say for sure. Two – three – When no one believes you, you begin to doubt yourself. I tried to say why they were against my history of Macedonia, but the embassy man laughed and said since when had the Greeks been afraid of history? Then in Greek he asked who I was working for. I became angry. He told the official I seemed hysterical, I remember the word, hysterical – I thought I was going to be sent back then, I was wet with fear, but the official referred the case and I started crying. I was humiliated.

Pause.

I brought you some grapes.

Pause.

I'm all right now.

Petra You teach?

Alexander I – I clean the streets.

Petra You wash the streets?

45

Alexander I pick up leaves, papers – there are a lot of dogs in the city.

Petra Alexander Karagy, descendant of Alexander the Great and the Bulgarian women who refuse to kneel, is cleaning the English streets of dogs?

Alexander Not dogs. Dog – eh.

Petra My son who was too proud to teach in a Greek university, who insisted he would teach our true history to all Macedonian children?

Alexander Everyone who comes here has a rich and bloody history on their shoulders. I look at people in the tube, all these histories raging in their heads.

Petra I sent you here to make allies of the English.

Alexander I spent months writing our history for my case. From memory: dates, massacres, the shifting of borders, the Macedonian Uprising, First Balkan War, Second Balkan War. I read it to the immigration officer. I was on the third page – 1913: the Treaty of Bucharest giving Southern Macedonia to Greece – when he stopped me. He had seven hundred and fifty cases after me. They've only had one civil war in England, and an endless parade of kings and queens, they speak one language, they don't even use the word history, they call it heritage.

Petra I said to go to the young people.

Alexander History for them is the childhood of their pop stars.

Petra Students love to demonstrate against injustice.

Alexander From here, it's only some obscure and convoluted corner of the world. Even for me – the more I wrote – the less it –

Petra It's your history.

Alexander Even in Macedonia it could feel like a prison. There is a wider world.

Petra You come from Macedonia.

Alexander Macedonia. Macedonia. Macedonia.

Petra Macedonia was your passion.

Alexander Because of you. You put me to bed with stories of Macedonian heroism. You sang me lullabies of blood and hatred.

Petra Your father was dead. I had to make a man out of you. You couldn't get enough of the stories.

Alexander Sometimes, from here, it looks like madness this obsession with Macedonia. Here, I've felt light, free.

Petra Light, free! It's never easy to be called by the history of your land. There are bad moments . . . When I was twenty-five, I was working for the radar station on Mount Hortiatis. I fell in love –

Alexander You don't have to tell me –

Petra – with an American officer. That was light, free. It went on many years. I didn't tell my family because the Americans had supported the other side in the civil war, but people always know. And the Colonels' Junta was forming. They had lists of all the Macedonian names. My uncle was arrested. When he came out months later, he showed me the torture marks: back, legs – and – (*She points.*) He said the equipment was too sophisticated for Greeks, he insisted it was American.

I married a pure Macedonian from Florina, a man who only cherished his land and his hatreds. My uncle led the wedding dance, all the village joined. Then – April 21, 1967 – the coup. They came to arrest your father – he died on the border, you know that – but I never told you that even as I mourned your father by day, at night I still dreamt of the soft skin of my American lover.

Alexander Please – Mamou –

Petra I had a son, conceived without pleasure.

Alexander Mamou – stop –

Petra But a Macedonian son and I suckled you on the pride of your family and of your land. My history became your history, that's how it goes.

Alexander It doesn't have to.

Petra You're nothing without your history.

Alexander From this distance, I've learned to look differently.

Petra I have understood that, Alexander. And I have decided we will have to go back.

Alexander Back?

Petra We have no choice.

Alexander Mamou – I can make a life here –

Petra It's worse than the body, they've broken your mind. You don't know who you are any more.

Alexander It'll take time, but I'll go on a computer course.

Petra No one can humiliate you in Macedonia. Your mind will clear.

Alexander I can write something from here.

Petra You're too far from your history here. There used to be a light in your face when I said Macedonia.

Alexander Mamou – I was beaten!

Petra I will guard you better.

Alexander They said they will kill me.

Pause.

Petra What kind of a life is there when you're a nobody, without a past, without a name, without a heart, a man who doesn't even cast a shadow, when maybe you're not even a man any more?

Alexander You would risk my life? Mamou!

Silence.

Petra I live for you: you're my only son.

Alexander I want to stay.

Petra You are Macedonian.

Alexander I had the courage to die then – you didn't want me to. Now I don't want to – I'm not sure of anything any more. I want to stay here – think more carefully –

Petra If you stay here, you will lose your land, and with Macedonia you will lose everything.

Alexander Why should I die for your obsessions? You dripped them into my food, the water I drank. You called it history, maybe it's only your anger.

Petra History is full of anger.

Alexander Because of mothers like you.

Petra You dare! The years I worked and plotted to get those fields back – I sacrificed everything so you could have your inheritance.

Alexander I may not want it.

Petra You don't know what you're saying.

Alexander I'm trying to tell the truth – it's hard with you, Mamou –

Petra You don't want to be Macedonian.

Alexander I want to make a life here.

Petra You don't want to be my son.

Alexander Mamou!

Petra My son can only be Macedonian!

Alexander I don't always have to do what you say.

Petra Sons obey their mothers.

Alexander Not in this country . . .

Petra We have nothing to do with this country – we are not part of its history.

Alexander It's interesting here.

Petra You are nobody here. Nobody!

Alexander What was I before? A cog in the wheel of a bloody history.

Petra They've washed out your heart, turned your liver to milk, they've ripped off your balls in this country. Come home before you disappear to mist.

Alexander No.

Petra This is your last chance, Alexander: come back to your Macedonia.

Alexander It's my life, Mamou –

Petra I gave you your life! I nourished your life – never to be a washed-up wreck on the English shores.

Alexander It's still my life.

Petra It may be your life, but it's not the life of my son. I brought you up to be a Macedonian. I don't know who you are any more, but I know this: you are not my son.

Alexander Mamou, you're tired, you haven't eaten.

Petra You don't even have the face of my son.

Alexander I'll come back tomorrow.

Petra Stranger –

Alexander You will understand – rest now.

Petra I curse you.

Alexander Mamou, don't do this. Please.

Petra Paul!

Alexander Mamou!

Paul comes.

Petra Take this man out. Don't ever let him come back. He doesn't know anything about my son. How could he? This man is not even a Macedonian.

SCENE ELEVEN

Same as before. Night. Cold. Petra, much weaker, and Shivan.
He kneels beside her.

Shivan If you don't eat, you will die.

Petra Last night, I heard the flutes of a procession. It was Alexander the God with a garland of leaves on his head. He moved through the rooms, came down here and then went out, through the barbed wire, onto the streets. And as the procession grew fainter and fainter

I knew Alexander the Great was abandoning me the way the god abandoned Antony. You know the story?

Shivan From Shakespeare: the music of a procession is heard by the soldiers through the streets, they say it's the god dancing out of the city. The next day, Antony loses the war . . .

Petra We had to learn a poem at school, it's in high Greek, but it's still beautiful: *Akouse me sukinesin . . . ta exaisia organa tou mistikou thiassou, ki apoxereta tin, tin Alexandria pou xaneis . . .*
  My son was at the back of the procession, dancing like a girl.

Shivan You love your son.

Petra I cursed him, Shivan.

Shivan I think he'll come back.

Petra When we give birth to our sons, we hold them more tightly than our daughters, we tremble when they're sick, we would die to protect them, but then we ask them to be men. All my life I've lived in terror he would die, but I cursed him because he wasn't willing to – Our history tells us to make sons that will fight – if that's not right, what have we been doing for hundreds of years? I came here with Macedonia clutched tight in my heart to find my son, but he wasn't any more the one I was looking for, the son I raised for my pride – now I have nothing in my heart.

Shivan You still love him.

Petra I cursed him.

Shivan Don't think about it now.

Petra He never disobeyed me, even questioned: you understand?

Shivan Yes.

Petra I wouldn't open my arms to the person in front of me, maybe if I had, my son would have come back –

Shivan Rest –

Petra I had to be mother and father to him, maybe a father would have understood.

Shivan I don't think so.

Petra I cursed my only son because he would not stay inside his history, but what is Macedonia to me without my son?

Shivan And then you will rest now.

Petra Nothing's solid any more.

Shivan You're dizzy from lack of food.

Petra When the god abandons you, Shivan, you must die.

Shivan I am a doctor, Petra. I take death very personally.

Petra Try not to be offended.

Shivan I am determined to make you eat: Alexander the Great never conquered Sri Lanka.

Petra That's because his Macedonian generals had already gone home.

Paul comes on, laden with bags.

Paul I've walked the city looking for this stuff. I shouldn't be doing it. It's not professional to be nice. I bought these as well.

He puts the bags on the floor and takes out some decorations, which he begins to hang across the room.

My New Year's resolution is to become tough.

Shivan looks through the bags. Ameena comes on, Shivan hands her a bag.

Ameena Cardamom. Flour. Sugar. Egg. Coconut milk.

Paul I even found a mortar and pestle. Is that what you were asking for?

Ameena Paul, you are good.

Paul Being good doesn't help you get on.

Ameena begins to grind the cardamom pods.

I didn't have enough money for some of these things. When I told the shopkeepers what it was for, they gave me stuff.
  I don't understand this country. One day they threaten to beat you up, next day – all this.

Shivan picks up a bag and leaves.

Shivan It is to do with the sense of fair play.

Ameena (*to Petra*) The smells of my country. (*She holds the bowl to Petra.*) Don't leave us . . . Please . . . don't leave me.

Aziz comes on, takes a bag.

Aziz Olives. Coriander. Lemon. Garlic. Two strands of saffron! Paul, you are a good angel.

Paul I'm changing at midnight.

Aziz (*to Petra*) I sprinkle this on the olives and you taste paradise.

Leon comes in, finds three mangoes, which he juggles expertly. Everyone laughs. Shivan now appears with a steaming pot.

Shivan Pol Sambal. With: grated coconut, grated onions, chilli powder, lime juice *and* string hoppers – I made those this morning – Paul did the rice. Also coming – steaming pepper water – special Tamil brew for great warriors only – even the Singhalese can't stomach it.

Leon starts playing. A moment of festivity. Simon walks in. Silence.

Simon There are no guards on the gates.

Paul They were refused extra pay tonight, they've gone on strike.

Simon Anyone could walk in.

Paul I called the office for reinforcement, but we agreed not many people will try to get into a detention centre on New Year's Eve.

Simon I'll hold you personally responsible if anything happens. What's all this?

Paul Everyone has cooked their favourite food for Mrs Karagy. It was Doctor Rajagopal's idea.

Simon You will need your strength, Mrs Karagy: we have lost all trace of your son. He was leafleting, then carrying a board – then nothing – disappeared.
My concern with finding your son is becoming unprofessional. I have a backlog of cases spilling off my desk. Meanwhile people continue to crawl through our borders like locusts. I can't spend any more official time on this, but I'm doing something exceptional. I'm giving you leave to remain here for six months on compassionate grounds. You're free, Mrs Karagy, you may go and look for your son.

Petra I have no son.

Simon I am certain he is alive and close.

Petra I never had a son.

55

Simon You're tired. I'll help you find your son in my free time, the little I have. I've found you a good hostel, I could take you there tonight.

Petra There is no son.

Simon Why are you doing this?

Petra I'm dying, I need to confess.

Simon The hunger strike was for the sake of your son.

Petra I wanted a better life, open a shop, own a little English land. But I've been disappointed in England: you have too many foreigners.

Simon What are you trying to tell me?

Petra I have to spell everything out? That's not very English, Mr Britten. I am a, what do you call it, yes, I'm an old bogus!

Simon I don't believe you.

Petra We don't always like the truth.

Simon (*shouts*) Why are you doing this to me?

Shivan Please. She's very weak.

Simon I'm never wrong!

Petra We all of us make mistakes, Mr English.

Simon Le Britten, please! It was a mistake to get too involved, I knew that. I don't know what game you're playing at. I've spent months looking for your son. I believed in you, I – liked you, I even wished you'd been my mother. Now you tell me I've wasted my precious time. Tonight, I was going to eat this pizza, I even brought you a piece and I was going to go out in the crowds and look for your son. I thought if you were up to it, you'd come with me – and when you got tired, I'd keep looking. I was going to ask you for the photographs.

Petra takes them out of a pocket and tears them up.

Petra I bought the pictures. You said it yourself: we're getting clever at this game.

Simon No one lasts in this job. I spend every hour of the day sifting through your lies, liars all of you, why can't you ever tell the truth!
I have news for the rest of you.
There's no way Aziz will be allowed to stay in this country. The Algerian government has assured Britain it has the country under control. There's a plane to Algiers the day after tomorrow.

Aziz I knew! When I go to sleep last night, I put my hands to my head: it wasn't there. I find it in an airport locker, smiling, but when I reach to put it back on, it's the wrong head. Please, Mr Britten – please –

Simon (*to Shivan*) Sri Lanka is at peace.

Shivan There was an attack on Tamils last week.

Simon We have hooligans in England.

Shivan I have a right to appeal.

Simon I will be at every one of your appeals.

Shivan Mr Le Britten, my wife was murdered.

Simon When there was real trouble in Sri Lanka we took in thousands of refugees. Why didn't you come in the eighties?

Shivan I was the youngest and most highly qualified Tamil doctor. I felt my expertise would keep me safe. I was also afraid Tamils would not get proper treatment from the Singhalese. The body has no evolutionary mechanism to heal itself of torture, and medicine is quite new at it. I treated Singhalese bomb victims as well. I don't actually know who burned down my house.

Simon The violence in Sri Lanka is negligible now.

Shivan You only mean it's not front page news.

Simon Other countries have priority. I've looked over all your statements, you are not a credible witness, Mr Rajagopal. (*He turns to Leon.*) You're too young to be in here. Your passport says you're forty, I think you're under age, I'm moving you to a children's hostel. As for you – (*He turns to Ameena.*) your story has been garbled from the start. You're on the first plane to Somalia next week. Don't all look at me like that, you've been here long enough and we need your beds.
  Happy New Year!
  (*to Petra*) My one mistake was to believe you, I won't make another one.

Petra Wait. Please.
  Don't leave like this.

  Simon hesitates, moves close, Petra grabs his hand.

I have something to say.
  Ameena, come here. (*She whispers to her.*)

  Ameena recoils in terror.

Do what I ask. Quick. (*to Shivan*) Don't let her escape.

  Ameena slowly begins to take off her blouse.
  All turn away except for Shivan and Petra.

Simon Good try, Mrs Karagy, but entrapment doesn't work with a man like me. Goodbye.

Petra Look at her, Mr England. LOOK!

  Simon looks – then turns away, shocked.

It is entrapment, but not by a pair of beautiful breasts.
  Look again. Count. You can't? Let me help you. Thirty-four cigarette burns on her front. Twenty-five on her back . . .

Shivan She's been here eight months. The doctor has given her the strongest tranquillisers he could find, but he hasn't once examined her.

Simon She screamed at the doctor, I have it on file.

Petra Did you ask why?

Simon I remember her first interview very well. The interpreter eventually got her to admit she'd been a prostitute.

Petra Where was the interpreter from?

Simon From Somalia, like her. Don't try to teach me my job.

Shivan Somalia hasn't had a government for the last eight years. There are twelve warring factions along tribal lines.

Simon I know all that!

Petra What faction was the interpreter?

Simon We're grateful to get someone from the same country, we pay a pittance!

Petra You put a young girl in front of two men, one an enemy, the other an official, and you asked her to tell you her life?

Simon If she was raped, all she had to do was say so, it would have put her in a different category.

Petra Three words. Do you know what it means to speak those words? Ameena, tell Mr Great Britain what happened.

Silence.

Go on, Ameena, say the words.

Ameena (*struggling*) I – was – (*inaudible*) They sur-round me in the street. Take me inside – dark – at first I don't see.

Eight. Eight men. I thought: for a beating – for names. I was prepared – for beating.

She laughs.

They don't want – names. For an hour, they shout – not at me – at each the other – who gets me first.

Petra She was a virgin, Mr Le Britten.

Ameena They even hit the other. I try to run then. Wrong.

She stops.

Then.

Many hours. Turned – turned over. Turned.

Pause.

Turned. They stop to smoke and crush cigarettes – on –

Petra She was seventeen. Go on, Ameena. Mr Le Britten wants credible testimony. Let's give him testimony.

Ameena Crush cigarettes. On.

Some. Others – start again. They – on my knees. Together now – they – everywhere. (*She gags slightly.*) Then. They throw me – on the street. It is light – sun.

My mother – No! I can't go home.

I walk – walk – North. I know North. Sleep anywhere. Many weeks. Into Ethiopia, trouble there too and a priest, I don't know, says Djibouti – there's a boat, takes me there on lorry, lots of people. I get on –

Petra I've seen women crawl into the gutter and die after one man, but she had the strength to keep walking, get on a lorry, keep going. She didn't lose that strength until she got here and two men called her a whore.

You still don't believe her? Ameena, take off your skirt.

Simon No!

Petra It's worse on her legs.

Simon Please!

Petra Do you believe her? Ameena –

Simon I believe her.

Petra Now you will swear to help her, you will get her a permanent leave to stay in England or she will take off her skirt, and there's another scar on –

Simon I'll reopen her case.

Petra Come to me, child. (*She cradles Ameena.*) Words are like medicine, they taste bad, but they help after. With every English word, you will tell your story more.

> *Petra subsides now, exhausted. Aziz is crying. Paul tidies the food, haphazardly.*
> *Alexander comes in, dishevelled, unsteady.*
> *Simon stares.*

Simon Who are you?

Alexander (*laughing, drunk*) No one.

Simon Mrs Karagy – surely this is –

Petra (*wearily*) I don't know who this is.

Alexander Mamou . . .

Petra Now the newspapers have my story of hunger strike, all these young men come here claiming I'm their mother. Crazy, lonely young men, even English.

Alexander Mamou!

Petra (*to Alexander*) If I were you, I wouldn't come in here. You may never get out. Save yourself.

Alexander *Ne moga.*

Petra *Spasi sebesi. Maxnise.*

Alexander *Nebes tvoata blagoslovia.*

Simon What are you saying?

Petra He's a crazy gypsy tinker, how do you ever let these people in? He thinks I'm a saint and he wants my blessing. If I don't give it, he'll bother us all night.

Paul Time to leave, son.

Alexander Mamou.

>   *Alexander goes to Petra, kisses her hand. She makes a blessing over him.*

Petra Go: live.

>   *Paul escorts Alexander out.*

Simon That was your son.

>   *Petra slumps slightly.*

That was your son. I have to get him arrested.

If I ask the police to chase an illegal immigrant on New Year's Eve, they'll laugh at me. Then it'll go on my file. I shouldn't have let him go. I'm supposed to be off duty. I'm so tired. That was your son. I'm always right – (*He looks at Ameena.*) No. Not always.

I haven't eaten all day. The pizza's getting cold. It's New Year's Eve.

My daughter's a cook on someone's yacht somewhere in the middle of the ocean. I've been working so hard, my place is a mess. I can't have someone do for me because they're all illegal. I had an Irish lady, she went back to Ireland, she sent me a picture of her new bungalow. There are all these dishes piling up in my sink.

>   *A pause. Leon starts playing the flute.*

Shivan Why don't you join us?

Simon I can't.

Shivan You would see us as too human?

Simon I never felt for England the way others do. Even at school I wanted to travel. I did love the history, the kings and queens, Disraeli, Churchill. I'm not narrow-minded, but I don't recognise anything any more. I feel dizzy. There's a lot of illness about. I need to sit down.

Petra Mr Le Britten.

Simon Simon, please.

Petra You're not a bad man.

Simon I'm making too many mistakes.

Petra Me too. About history. I've been walled, like you. But you will make Ameena British, yes, and Shivan too, he loves the language, and Aziz? History shifts, Simon, we can't hold it. And now, when we turn to you, don't cover your eyes and think of the kings and queens of England. Look at us: we are your history now.

Petra subsides. Simon keeps hold of her hand. Shivan takes the pulse of the other hand, then closes her eyes. Leon places the three mangoes on her lap. Paul comes back in. He starts to cry. Straight into:

EPILOGUE

Spring light. Alexander sits, wrapped in a blanket. He looks rough. Henry and Anna come on.

Henry Teacher!

Alexander starts, then bows his head as if it's not him. Anna thrusts a paper in his hand.

Anna Five A-levels. Two A-stars. Henry has to retake GCSEs I'm going to help him. He has a gardening job for the summer. Chocolate? (*She unwraps a chocolate, gives it to Alexander.*) The best university in England wants Anna Kadare. At the interview, I told them I wanted to be a Biological Historian with a special interest in genes. You know that animals suffer something called tonic immobility – it is the same as what Freud calls hysterical paralysis – you freeze, can't move. Now they think it's genetic, because for animals it's safer not to move from the hunter. But what about humans? When the Serbs came to our village, we all froze. Hysterical paralysis. What makes people freeze at certain moments of history? Hysterical paralysis? Historical paralysis? Is it genetic? And if we understand it, can we prevent it?

One of the Dons laughed at a word I used and I froze with fury. I got up to kick the chair at him. Then I sat down, smiled and I asked him: would you call that movement hysterical? – historical? – an evolutionary defence gone wrong? – random violence? The most important, of course, was the movement when I sat down again. That's called change, but I couldn't tell them that. At the end, they said they were amazed to find someone with such ideas and they couldn't fault me on my biology. You understand what I'm looking for? Not this country's history, or the one I came from, but the common mechanism –

Alexander nods, smiles.

I knew you would. I've already planned my thesis, it will be controversial. Ali's gone back . . . He got involved with the Islamist group in Finsbury Park, they taught him to shoot, he wouldn't talk to us.

Pause.

Remember your crying lessons? I pretended not to understand, but when I got back to that filthy hotel room

64

where we all lived, I'd do hours of crying homework.
And then I could study. Here: white chocolate with
caramel and almonds inside.
  We're going for a walk.
  Come with us.

  Alexander shakes his head.

Henry Remember, teacher, you once ask me to find
something I like about this country. It is very hard, but
I decide I like the parks.

  Pause.

My name is Abdillahi Hassan.

Anna No one can pronounce it, so we still call him
Henry.
  Come on, teacher, come and walk with us in an
English park.